PREFAB HOMES

Elisabeth Blanchet

Published in Great Britain in 2016 by Shire Publications Ltd, part of Bloomsbury Publishing Plc
PO Box 883, Oxford, OX1 9PL, UK
1385 Broadway, 5th Floor, New York, NY 10018, USA
E-mail: shire@shirebooks.co.uk   www.shirebooks.co.uk

Every attempt has been made by the Publishers to secure the appropriate permissions for materials reproduced in this book. If there has been any oversight we will be happy to rectify the situation and a written submission should be made to the Publishers.

A CIP catalogue record for this book is available from the British Library.

Shire Library no. 788.   ISBN-13: 978 0 74781 357 6
PDF e-book ISBN: 978 1 78442 029 1
ePub ISBN: 978 1 78442 028 4

Elisabeth Blanchet has asserted her right under the Copyright, Designs and Patents Act, 1988, to be identified as the author of this book.

Designed by Tony Truscott Designs, Sussex, UK
Typeset in Garamond Pro and Gill Sans.
Printed in China through World Print Ltd.

16 17 18 19 20   11 10 9 8 7 6 5 4 3 2

COVER IMAGE
Cover design and photography by Peter Ashley. Front cover: Prefab on the Excalibur Estate, Catford, South London. Back cover: Festival of Britain book of matches, collection of Peter Ashley.

TITLE PAGE IMAGE
LCC prefabs in Kennington, London, 1973.

CONTENTS PAGE IMAGE
The AIROH 'back bedroom' at St Fagans has two windows onto the back garden and a wall with original fitted cupboards and wardrobe.

ACKNOWLEDGEMENTS
The author would like to thank Ian Abley, Graham Burton, Howard Davies, Selim Korycki, James Solway, Luc Trémoulet, Sonia Zhuravlyova for their help with research.

The author is very grateful to all those who supplied photographs or allowed her to photograph their homes. Thanks go to Jim Blackender, Matthew Bristow, BRE (Building Research Establishment), Nick Davis, Peggie Dobbs, Tom Dolan, Great Yarmouth Mercury, Huf Haus, Dave Miller, Alan Page, Christine Rich, St Astier Consulting Contractors, Lord West of Spithead, Andrew Whittuck and David Willis.

Photographs and illustrations are reproduced with the kind permission of: Alamy, page 6; Jim Blackender, page 39 (top); BRE - AP294, page 23, reproduced with permission; Matthew Bristow, University of London, page 47; Russell Butcher, page 48 (top); Nick Davis, pages 21 (bottom), and 52; Peggie Dobbs, pages 33, and 40; Tom Dolan, page 46; Getty Images, pages 10,12, 25, 30; Great Yarmouth Mercury, reproduced with permission, page 42; Huf Haus, page 57; Imperial War Museum (H 39466), page 9; Dave Miller, pages 43, and 61 (top); National Archives, page 20; Alan Page, pages 29, and 39 (bottom); Christine Rich, page 44; St Astier Consulting Contractors, page 22 (bottom); Lord West of Spithead, page 41; Andrew Whittuck page 61 (bottom); David Willis, pages 21 (top), and 62.

All others are from the author's collection.

Shire Publications is supporting the Woodland Trust, the UK's leading woodland conservation charity, by funding the dedication of trees.

CONTENTS

INTRODUCTION

THE FIRST WORLD War provided a new impetus to improve social housing in Britain, when the poor health of many new army recruits was noted with alarm. This led to a campaign known as Homes Fit for Heroes. In 1919 the government requested councils to provide housing, helping them to do so through subsidies. Under the Housing Act 1919, half a million new houses were planned. As the economy weakened in the early 1920s, however, funding had to be cut, and only 213,000 homes were completed under the Act's provisions.

The 1919 Act – often known as the 'Addison Act' after its author, Dr Christopher Addison, the Minister of Health – was a significant step forward in housing provision. Housing became a national responsibility, and local authorities were given the task of developing new accommodation for working people.

Many houses were built for artisans, clerks, and the semi-skilled working classes, who could now afford to leave the inner cities. The world's largest planned suburb was built at Becontree in Essex, while good quality suburban housing was planned around Leeds, Birmingham, Liverpool, Manchester, and Sheffield.

By the 1920s, not much had been done to resolve the problem of inner-city slums. However, this changed with the new Housing Act of 1930, which obliged local councils to clear all slums and provided subsidies to rehouse their inhabitants. This single act led to the building of 700,000 new homes. Under the provisions of the inter-war housing acts, local councils built a total of 1.1 million homes.

Still, the Homes Fit for Heroes promise failed to materialise entirely, as Grandad, from the BBC's *Only Fools and Horses*, points out in his description of the wartime government policy: 'They promised us homes fit for heroes; we got heroes fit for homes!' By the end of the Second World War, Winston Churchill and his government had new heroes to welcome back and house, this time in prefabs.

WINSTON CHURCHILL'S PROMISE OF 500,000 EMERGENCY HOMES

Sunday 26 March 1944. The end of the Second World War is finally approaching, as Prime Minister Winston Churchill points out in his BBC broadcast speech, 'Our Greatest Effort is Coming'. In a part of his speech, he anticipates the huge post-war housing shortage and the reconstruction effort: 'But now about a million homes have been destroyed or grievously damaged by the fire of the enemy. This offers a magnificent opportunity for rebuilding and replanning, and while we are at it we had better make a clean sweep of all those areas of which our civilization should be ashamed.'

Churchill declared a new war, but this time, on poor housing. Using military words, he unveiled his strategy:

> The first attack must evidently be made upon houses which are damaged, but which can be reconditioned into proper dwellings … The second attack on the housing problem will be made by what are called the prefabricated, or emergency, houses. On this the Minister of Works, Lord Portal, is working wonders. I hope we may make up to half a million of these, and for this purpose not only plans but actual preparations are being made during the war on a nationwide scale. Factories have been assigned,

Winston Churchill delivering a speech at the BBC during the Second World War.

the necessary set-up is being made ready, materials are being ear-marked as far as possible, the most convenient sites will be chosen, the whole business is to be treated as a military evolution handled by the government with private industry harnessed to its service.

In Churchill's speech, there is a hint of fear. Imagine an army of demobilised men with no one to fight and with no homes or employment – housing these men and their families was a priority. The Blitz and the continuous bombings of ports and big industrial cities destroyed 3 million homes, and by March 1944 they were still more raids to come. Vicious weapons, such as the V-2 rockets, relentlessly damaged the country, killing civilians, and wiping out their homes.

When the Blitz was called off in May 1941, 43,000 people had been killed and 1.4 million had been made homeless. A quarter of British dwellings had been destroyed or severely damaged when the Germans finally stopped their attack in March 1945. Most of the bombings affected working-class areas – homes and factories were the Germans' prime targets. But it wasn't just London that suffered; many other British cities were attacked too.

In order to fight the enemy, Britain was transformed into a war machine. All industries shared the same target: to win the war. In March 1944, the UK was still producing ammunition and aircraft. There was going to be a surplus and the conversion of factories for mass production of prefabricated houses appeared to be a good solution.

The Homes Fit For Heroes policy, started in 1919, continued during the Second World War, but was slowed down by the diminished labour force and the lack of materials. The construction rate was almost a tenth of what it had been before 1939 and the maintenance of existing homes was not kept up. Living conditions declined, leaving people without glass in their windows or with tarpaulin on their roofs.

During the war, the issue of housing was first raised in the King's Speech to Parliament on 11 November 1942. Churchill formed a cross-party committee, under the chairmanship of Sir George Burt, to address the problem. The committee sent British engineers to America to find out how the United States intended to address its needs for post-war housing. The outcome of the Burt Committee was a favourable view of prefabricated housing as a solution to the housing shortage, and Churchill announced this in his Temporary Housing Programme: 'All these emergency houses will be publicly owned and it will not rest with any individual tenant to keep them in being after they have served their purpose of tiding over the return of the fighting men and after permanent dwellings are available. As much thought has been and will be put into this plan as was put into the invasion of Africa.'

The plan was to build 500,000 'new technology' temporary houses as soon as the war ended, and this passed into law as the Housing (Temporary Accommodation) Act, 1944. Over the next four years, 300,000 prefab houses were to be built in Britain, with a structural lifetime of between ten to fifteen years.

To achieve Churchill's ambitious housing plan, the Ministry of Works (MoW) created research institutes to work on the design of the new houses. People had high expectations and felt their homes should contain the latest electric appliances, as well as indoor toilets and bathing facilities. The government took this into account and as well as installing a fridge and a gas cooker, it worked to build a house that contained a coal fire and a back boiler to create central heating and a constant supply of hot water. In 1951 about a third of British households were still without a plumbed-in bath, so this was luxury.

The government invested in a model temporary steel bungalow. Following an announcement about the prototype by Lord Portal on 8 February 1944, the prototype became known as the 'Portal bungalow'. Designed by the architects C. J. Mole and A. W. Kenyon, it was constructed by hand by the motor manufacturer Briggs Motor Bodies of Dagenham and the Pressed Steel Company of Cowley.

By May 1944 the first prototype was ready for public display at the Tate Gallery in London, and it was shown in Edinburgh in June. It was radically different from inter-war social housing. Its flat roof and rectangular shape reminded people of Hollywood villas they had seen at the pictures.

The Portal bungalow impressed the Tate Gallery visitors: the level of fittings and equipment was far beyond what people had expected. Reactions to the exterior of the prototype were rather mixed, however. Knowing that a car factory had built the prototype, people asked why the Portal bungalow didn't have any windscreen wipers!

After the exhibition, comments were made on how to improve the Portal and its design was revised. The ceiling was raised in height to 7.5 feet, and two doors were added – one to the kitchen leading into the garden, and one from the hallway directly into the living room. The original idea that each prefab would have a shed was unfortunately scrapped.

'Portal prototype' or 'Churchill House' (see page 15) exhibited in Edinburgh, 1944.

DELIVERING PALACES FOR THE PEOPLE

AFTER THE END of the war, and after the disappointment of the Homes Fit For Heroes programme, the government knew it couldn't fail again to provide adequate housing. For social, logistical, and even political and ideological reasons, prefabricated houses appeared to be the best option. A huge amount of servicemen were expected to return to Britain with higher expectations than after the Great War. Some would have had access to education through their time with the forces and aspire to a better standard of living. Moreover, after all they had given to their country, they could expect a reward – a nice and comfortable house to come back to.

The Temporary Housing Programme's objective was to provide a large number of houses that could be built without slowing down the building of permanent housing. In August 1944, Henry Willink, the Minister of Health, announced: 'We felt that it was of the first importance that this project should not delay the building of permanent houses, and, consequently, that it should make the minimum demand on the building industry. That consideration pointed to a type of building, so far as possible, factory made ... whereas it is usually reckoned that it takes 100,000 building operatives to build 100,000 houses in a year, the building labour force required for 100,000 of these bungalows is not more than 8,000 to 10,000.'

There was a lack of skilled labour in the building industry after the war, but prefabs were quick and easy to assemble.

Opposite: In May 1944 the press photographed an ex-serviceman and his family viewing a Churchill all-steel house. Here, the housewife discovers the gas fridge in the prefab kitchen.

This gave jobs to servicemen coming back from the war as well as to the unemployed. German and Italian prisoners of war were also used as free labour. Eddie O'Mahony, who has lived in a prefab in Catford, south-east London, since 1946 recalls: 'The estate was built by German prisoners of war and very well assembled. Winter 1946 was particularly tough. I woke up one morning and the snow had reached the level of the garden fence. I got scared the flat roof wouldn't resist the weight, but it did! And I still praise the Germans for their good work.'

Keeping men busy by giving them jobs was necessary to maintain social cohesion. But what would happen to the women who had replaced them in factories during the war? The detached prefabs and its mod cons were designed to tempt women back home, encouraging them to start families. 'And I have every hope and a firm resolve that several hundred thousand of our young men will be able to

Hector Murdoch's historic homecoming (with a prefab in the background) in 1946 became one of the war's most famous images.

Eddie O'Mahony has lived at his Uni-Seco since 1946. The porch at the side entrance is his own addition.

marry several hundred thousand of our young women and make their own four-year plan,' said Churchill in his 1944 BBC speech.

Another job was convincing people that prefabs were more than improved Anderson shelters or Nissen huts. Some thought prefabs were a waste of time and resources. George Bernard Shaw referred to the Portal prefab as the 'Heartbreak House' and the 'Damn Tin Can'. The architect Walter Segal made a constructive criticism: he suggested that the prefabs should be erected opposite proposed permanent housing sites, so that communities could stay together and move across the road in due course.

A policy of prefab propaganda was set in place. The BBC broadcast programmes analysing the virtues of prefabrication. Public discussions, like the one at the Tate, were regularly held to promote prefabs, but also to involve the public in improving their design. Many publications aimed at architects and the general public were written at the end of the war to promote the idea of prefabrication. Among them was a large survey started in 1943 by the Directorate of Post-war Building of the MoW. Its aim was to assess the range of prefabrication in countries such as Germany, France, the United States, and elsewhere. America, which had never broken with the timber housing tradition, as well as Sweden, were of particular interest. Famous architects Walter Gropius and Konrad Wachsmann were asked to provide information on their own prefabs. The results of the Survey of Prefabrication were published by the MoW in 1945. At the time the document appeared to be the most extensive and carefully researched comparative study of prefabrication undertaken anywhere in the world.

Architect Bernard Cox published a thirty-six-page pamphlet, *Prefabricated Homes*, featuring British, American, and Swedish prefabs and prototypes. Fellow architect Hugh Casson recommended in his book, *Homes by the Million*, the replication of the US model for the reconstruction of Europe. He concluded that post-war housing had to be the responsibility of the state, that the construction industry had to be reorganised to increase prefabrication production, and that the new houses had to have facilities for communal use.

Eleven different types of prefabs were manufactured under the Temporary Housing Programme from 1944–8. All prefabs were constructed from prebuilt panels, either attached to a prefabricated wood or metal frame, or constructed from self-supporting panels. The government estimated that the nation would need 3 to 4 million new homes. The Portal prototype was also sometimes called the 'Churchill House', as the Prime Minister was so enthusiastic about these houses. There is even a short

Hugh Casson's *Homes by the Million* gives an account of the housing methods used by the United States from 1940 to 1945.

film, by British Pathé, showing Mrs Churchill visiting a prefab.

However, despite the ingenuity of its design and the fact that they were largely handmade to show what could be mass-produced, the Portal prefabs proved to be too complicated to manufacture, as the steel and the engineering skills needed to complete them were still restricted to war-related services for the foreseeable future.

More types were then produced: the Arcon Mark V, the Uni-Seco, the Tarran, the Aluminium (the AIROH), the American (also called the USA), the Phoenix, the Spooner, the Universal, the Orlit, the Isle of Lewis special houses, and the Miller. All approved prefabs had to have a minimum floor size of 635 square feet (59 square metres) and be a maximum of 7.5 square feet (2.3 square metres) wide to allow transportation by road.

PORTAL (OR CHURCHILL HOUSE)

The Portal prefab was designed by C. J. Male, Arthur Kenyon, and Dr Stradling in 1944. It had a living room, two bedrooms, a kitchen, a bathroom, a separate toilet, an entrance hall, and a porch at the front door. A small separate shed was also provided to the rear. Being the first to be built, the Portal remains the most famous prefab, although it was never mass-produced. Its design rested largely on the use of pressed steel. Only prototypes appear to have been constructed despite a government intention to have manufactured 50,000, and no known examples of this prefab remain today. After spending £92,000, the government cancelled the project, but the Portal prefab set the standard by which all subsequent prefabs were designed, with only minor variations.

ARCON MK V

Arcon (derived from 'Architectural Consultants') was the name of a group that came together in April 1943 to

An Arcon V on the Treberth and Bishpool Estate, Newport.

design asbestos-clad demountable prefabs. It included the architects Edric Neel, Jim Gear, Raglan Squire, Rodney Thomas, and the construction firm Taylor Woodrow. Mainly because of the different stages it went through (Mark I to IV came before the V), the Arcon was seen as the most architecturally sophisticated prefab. At the same time, it is a very simple design and it used traditional, rather than innovative, materials. They were easy to transport and assemble, and thanks to a combination of good design and fine co-ordination, they were a success. An Arcon Mk V is exhibited at the Rural Life Centre in Farnham, Surrey, and three are still standing in Newport, Wales.

ALUMINIUM BUNGALOW

The Aluminium bungalow was also called the B2 or the AIROH (Aircraft Industries Research Organisation on Housing). It emerged out of the need for aircraft manufacturers to diversify in the immediate post-war

period. AIROH was an organisation that gathered more than a dozen aircraft manufacturers together. The B2 bungalow, designed by Morrison's Engineering Company, came complete with all fixtures and fittings already in place, including the standard MoW kitchen and bathroom units. The B2 was also the only prefab that was painted in the factory. Aluminium bungalows were the most numerous, the most expensive (some of the aluminium had to be imported, but also the most prefabricated. They were designed with a life-expectancy of about ten years. None have survived beyond the 1990s, but there is a reconstructed B2 exhibited at the St Fagans National History Museum in Cardiff, Wales.

This AIROH at the St Fagans National History Museum may be the last aluminium prefab in Britain. It was one of forty that were built in Llandinam Crescent in Cardiff in 1948.

UNI-SECO

The Uni-Secos were created in 1945. They were the most numerous after the B2 prefabs and the Arcons. With their flat roofs and their corner windows, they looked

A Uni-Seco with a side entrance on the Excalibur Estate, Catford.

A Uni-Seco with a middle entrance in Peckham.

strikingly modern. The main difference between the Uni-Seco and the other types of prefab was its flexibility. The company designed a kit of parts that could be assembled in various combinations to suit the location and avoid a repetitive appearance. For example, there were two distinctive types of Uni-Secos: one with a middle entrance and one with a corner entrance. In south-east London, both types were cleverly combined on the Excalibur Estate in Catford, and there are still a few Uni-Secos standing in Peckham, Nunhead, and Dulwich.

TARRAN

Robert Tarran from Tarran Industries of Hull (and Edinburgh, Leeds, and Dundee) built these prefabs from

the late 1930s to the early 1940s. The design of the Tarran was almost identical to the Uni-Seco. The only difference was the roof: the Tarran's was traditionally pitched, made of asbestos concrete, and the outside was cladded with concrete panels. This made the Tarran bungalows particularly heavy (14 tons each) and probably explains why they were mainly erected in the north of England and Scotland, close to the factory that manufactured them. Tarran produced three different versions and a few hundred of them are still occupied in North Derbyshire.

A Tarran in Old Brampton, Chesterfield, North Derbyshire.

An American prefab, probably the last one standing in the UK, in Lewes, East Sussex.

AMERICAN

This prefab was also called the USA. Designed in the 1940s by the Tennessee Valley Authority and other American defence programmes, it was the only prefab to be imported. Its layout was inspired by the Portal prefab. These bungalows were slightly smaller than the

other prefabs, and they generally had a shorter life because their construction was unsuitable for the British climate. They were all demolished by the mid-1960s but there is still one on a farm in East Sussex, desperately looking for a home.

SPOONER

Designed by J. L. Spooner for Universal Engineering Ltd in 1946, the Spooner was built using plywood panels placed between timber frames, despite the national timber shortage. The roof was made of felt-covered plywood. Some were also clad in aluminium alloy sheets or asbestos-clad cement. A version was exhibited at the Tate Gallery at the beginning of 1945. No remaining examples are known.

UNIVERSAL

A Spooner prefab, clearly showing its panel construction.

The Universal was manufactured in 1946 by the Universal Housing Company Ltd, Rickmansworth. Its steel frames and roof trusses were clad with asbestos cement. An example can be found at the Chiltern Open Air Museum, Chalfont St Giles, Buckinghamshire.

Universal prefab at the Chiltern Open Air Museum, Buckingham-shire.

PHOENIX

Designed in the 1930s by the architects of constructors John Laing, Robert McAlpine, and Henry Boot plc, the Phoenix prefab resembles a traditional cottage. With its panelled

Phoenix prefab still standing on Wake Green Road, Birmingham.

Phoenix 'Isle of Lewis type' prefab in Plasterfield, Stornoway, Isle of Lewis.

Orlit House Type 2, City of York.

timber front door and a slightly pitched roof, the Phoenix looked very cosy. Some survive in good condition in Moseley, Birmingham, and were listed in 1998 by English Heritage.

A specially insulated version was designed for use on Scotland's Isle of Lewis. Known as the 'Isle of Lewis type', fifty of them were built and still stand.

ORLIT

The Orlit was created in 1940 by Czech architect Erwin Katona, who came to the UK in 1938. It is a two-storey precast, reinforced concrete prefab. The design was produced in Scotland by the Orlit Company, resulting in most houses being located there. There are a few left in Sutton, Surrey.

MILLER

Scottish company Miller built their eponymous house in 1946. The timber roof was clad with asbestos-cement sheets. The internal walls, made of hardboard attached to timber frames, were the most prefabricated element in the Miller. A few remaining examples are known in Scotland.

This photograph of a Miller house in Port Seton, Midlothian, Scotland, was taken in 1980.

ALUMINIUM BUNGALOWS

Cost: £1,610 per unit; in total: £87,745,000
Number manufactured: 54,500
Where: Bristol
Material used: Aluminium

AMERICAN (OR USA)

Cost: £663 per unit; in total: £5,610,000
Number manufactured: 8,462
Where: East and north-west London
Material used: Timber frame, fibreboard, cement sheets

ARCON MK V

Cost: £1,085 per unit; in total: £42,162,000
Number manufactured: 38,859
Where: Newport, South Wales, Bristol, London
Materials used: Asbestos, cement panels, steel frames

ISLE OF LEWIS TYPE

Cost: £2,000 per unit; in total: £100,000
Number manufactured: 50
Where: Isle of Lewis
Main material used: Concrete

MILLER

Cost: £1,139 per unit; in total: £114,000
Number manufactured: 100
Where: Scotland
Main material used: Concrete construction

ORLIT

Cost: £1,202 per unit; in total: £307,000
Number manufactured: 255
Where: Mainly Scotland, Surrey
Main material used: Concrete

PHOENIX

Cost: £1,200 per unit; in total: £2,914,000
Number manufactured: 2,428
Where: Moseley, Birmingham
Main material used: Asbestos-clad

PORTAL (OR CHURCHILL HOUSE)

Cost: £92,000
Number manufactured: A few prototypes were constructed but none of them mass-produced
Where: UK
Main material used: Steel

SPOONER

Cost: £1,079 per unit; in total: £2,158,000
Number manufactured: 2,000
Where: Colchester
Main material used: Plywood

TARRAN

Costs (there were three types of Tarrans):
£1,022 per unit (1,015 manufactured); total cost: £1,037,000
£1,147 per unit (11,000 manufactured); total cost: £12,617,000
£1,126 per unit (6,999 manufactured); total cost: £7,881,000
Number manufactured: 19,014
Where: Mainly northern England, Scotland
Main material used: Concrete

UNI-SECO

Cost: £1,131 per unit; in total: £32,798,000
Number manufactured: 28,999
Where: Catford in South London

UNIVERSAL

Cost: £1,218 per unit; in total: £2,436,000
Number manufactured: 2,000
Where: Buckleigh Road, Streatham, South London
Main material used: Asbestos cement attached to timber-framed panels
NB: There might be other places where prefabs once stood.

The 'service unit' or 'heart unit' was standard to all prefabs, except for the imported American, and was the most innovative creation of the MoW. The unit consisted of a prefabricated kitchen that backed on to a bathroom, prebuilt in a factory to an agreed size. The water and waste pipes, as well as electrical distribution, were all in the same place and easy to install.

Innovation didn't stop at the kitchen door: ingenuity was also put into the heating system. Every prefab had a coal fire and a back boiler that created central heating and a constant supply of hot water. This was a luxury at the time, as most people were used to outside toilets and tin baths.

The design of the service unit was inspired by what was called the Frankfurt Kitchen in Germany. It was a milestone in domestic architecture and was considered the forerunner of modern fitted kitchens, for it was created, in 1926, to increase efficiency and to be built at low cost. It was designed by Austrian architect Margarete Schütte-Lihotzky for Ernst May's social housing project in Frankfurt.

In 1943, the Selection Engineering Company in London appointed the Hungarian émigré George Féjer

Two women inspect the kitchen inside a newly built prefabricated house, around 1950.

to design the post-war prefab kitchen. He was a leading figure in introducing new ideas about kitchen design and appliances: 'I got involved in kitchen design because here was an area where all the arts and techniques of living, design, and manufacture seemed to meet, and where unsolved problems were legion, and where so many new products were evidently waiting to be born.'

Féjer's design was used in all the prefabs and when *The Sociological Review* examined the high level of satisfaction expressed by housewives, it found that the modernity of the kitchen and bathroom was one of the main factors, together with low ceilings and a compact plan, which ensured that heating costs were affordable, compared with traditional housing. Catford Uni-Seco resident Eddie O'Mahony recalls: 'At first I wasn't sure I wanted to live in a prefab – I had spent too many hours in Nissen huts during the war – but my wife Ellen immediately loved its mod cons: the refrigerator, the gas stove, the bathroom and space for the pram in the hallway!'

'They (the emergency houses) are, in my opinion, far superior to the ordinary cottage as it exists today. Not only have they excellent baths, gas or electric kitchenettes and refrigerators, but their walls carry fitted furniture – chests of drawers, hanging cupboards, and tables which today it would cost eighty pounds to buy,' opined Churchill in 1944. There were nice little design touches too: most of the prefabs came pre-painted in magnolia, with gloss-green on the door trimmings and skirting boards.

Churchill had hopes for half a million temporary bungalows, but only a little more than 150,000 could be provided without taking

A prefab kitchen was fitted with modern equipment such as a gas fridge, cooker, copper (washing machine), fitted shelves and cupboards, and constant hot water.

The original cupboards in the AIROH's kitchen at St Fagans National History Museum.

up resources needed for permanent dwellings. The 1944 Housing Act authorised the expenditure of £150 million. The MoW contracted individual suppliers for materials and components, and construction firms to erect the houses, while local authorities obtained sites and prepared off-site services and roads.

In the instruction manual produced by the government, local authorities were advised on layouts, maintenance, selection of tenants, and management. In Parliament, the Commons stipulated the guidance the manual should give: 'The authority will choose the tenants, fix and receive the rents, manage the property, and keep it in repair. The authority will make an annual payment to the Ministry of Health of an amount to be determined' (*Commons Hansard*).

It was up to the local authorities to decide where prefabs would be erected. Occasionally, just a few bungalows would replace bomb-damaged homes and would fill the holes on a street façade between traditional houses. This was what happened in London areas such as Peckham, Nunhead, Dulwich, Elephant and Castle, Shoreditch, and others. Estates of prefabs (from fifty units to hundreds) also blossomed all over the country on brown and greenfield sites, and on vacant and derelict land in cities and rural areas. Unfortunately, there is no national record or map of where all the post-war prefabs were erected. While some records remain, other locations have been lost or are buried deep in council archives.

Local councils decided who should live in the prefabs, with priority being given to people with children or with special medical needs. In most areas, when families had more than two children, especially if they were of opposite sex, they had to move out as councils wouldn't allow them to share the same bedroom. Allocated according to need, there were also some exceptions. If you suffered from an illness or were disabled, you could get a prefab even if you didn't have children. Peggie Dobbs, from Newport, remembers: 'We (my husband and I) got our prefab because I had had TB during the war. I remember the neighbours were suspicious about the way we had got the prefab as we hadn't children yet!' In 1946, Alan Page, who also had TB, lived with his mother, father, and sister in a rented room. His parents applied to get a prefab and had priority over other families because of Alan's medical condition. He recalls: 'I remember when my mother got the letter.

Two Uni-Secos between pre-war buildings in Nunhead, southeast London.

She was so happy. I was nine. The prefab really suited us.'

A few estates were also built especially for key workers such as the one in Birmingham for the City Police Force. Lord Kinnock lived in an Arcon prefab in Tregedar, South Wales from 1948 till 1962, and recalls: 'The prefabs were for the most committed and hardworking of the working class. It is because the prefabs where I grew up were a tiny estate all for key workers: an ambulance driver, a dental mechanic, my mother was a district nurse, the deputy manager of a local manufacturer, two policemen and other mechanics, people whose existence was absolutely vital for the operation of the area in general.'

Prefabs were social housing and the councils would set the rent. For example, the Page family's rent in Newport was 14 shillings and tuppence per week in 1946, while on the Excalibur Estate in Catford, rents were 17 shillings per week in 1947.

Letter from the County Borough of Newport, granting a 'temporary prefabricated bungalow' to the Page family.

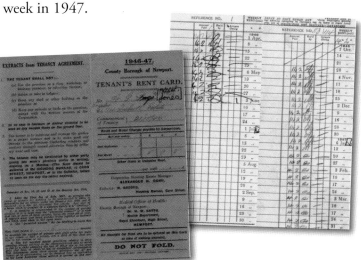

The Page family's rent card, Newport, 1946.

PREFAB LIFE

ALL PREFABS CAME with a comfort most people had never had in their life. A survey conducted in 1950 by the Women's Group on Public Welfare found that of the 249 housewives interviewed, for half, the prefab was the first home that they had run for themselves, having previously been forced to share accommodation. Compared with the living conditions working-class families endured before and during the Second World War, the prefab was an ideal home. 'They were a luxury,' Eddie O'Mahony comments. 'In 1946, you had to be very very posh and have plenty of money to have a house with a toilet inside. Then a bathroom ... I had been used to queuing up at the municipal baths ... so, to find a bathroom inside was magic and a hot towel rail – I had never heard of that!'

The same 1950 survey revealed that housewives found daily tasks such as cooking, washing up, cleaning, childcare, and laundry easier in the prefab than in their previous accommodation, and when moved into permanent housing, about half of those interviewed found cleaning the house and laundry more difficult and time-consuming.

During his 'Our Greatest Effort is Coming' speech at the BBC in 1944, Churchill had declared: 'Moreover, for the rest of the furniture, standard articles will be provided and mass-produced so that no heavy capital charge will fall upon the young couples or others who may become tenants of the houses.' He kept his promises and for the first time, these goods were supplied by the government.

Opposite:
A mother sees her daughter off to school from their prefab home in Bromley-by-Bow, a heavily blitzed area of East London, in 1946.

Prefabs had so many fitted cupboards and shelves that residents didn't have to buy storage furniture. No space was wasted; cupboards were fitted in every available space with the same kind of ingenuity one would find in a caravan. Kitchens also came equipped with pots and pans.

Eddie O'Mahony's bathroom with the original shelving and hot rail for towels, Catford.

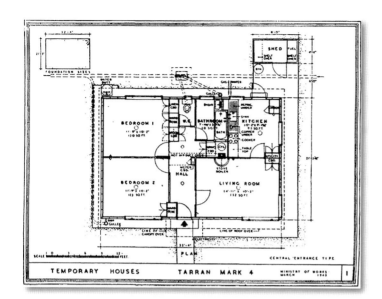

Tarran Mark 4 blueprint, Ministry of Works, 1943.

Just after the war, about a quarter of the British population didn't have a mains electricity supply. The government had to produce a booklet, *Electric Service in Temporary Houses*, to enable new residents to take advantage of the 'efficiency' and 'freedom' electricity could bring to their lives. Each prefab had six electric power points: two in the kitchen, two in the living room, and one in each bedroom. In the kitchen, the cooker was more advanced than those that most people had been used to: it had an oven, a separate grill, two hotplates, and a 'SIM' control for simmering.

Another revolutionary item was the refrigerator. It had the capacity of 3 cubic feet, a volume the government considered 'ample for the storage of perishable food needed for an average household'. The residents were advised to use it all year long and not only in hot weather. The fridge, as well as the boiler and the cooker, were connected to gas or electricity.

Electric services manual given to Peggie Dobbs when she was allocated her Newport prefab in 1946.

ELECTRIC SERVICE IN **TEMPORARY HOUSES**

Prefabs were cold in winter. The living room was heated by a multi-fuel stove. Hot air, ducted from the stove or the boiler, was the only source of heat for the hallway and the two bedrooms. Joyce Cramp, who lives in a Tarran in North Derbyshire, remembers the first years in her prefab: 'I moved in in 1955. I have loved every minute I have been here but they were so cold. Every night I put cloths around as the water used to run down the wallpaper. When I took them off in the morning, they were froze solid.' Most of the remaining prefabs now have central heating, mainly thanks to the Decent Homes Programme set in place by the Labour government in 2004.

Despite the cold, the prefab enabled a new way of living. Its design was a first, and broke down all assumptions about building new homes. It provided single-storey living, all mod cons, and no wasted space such as parlours or grandiose hallways. The notion of 'good design' in the home was introduced with the prefabs: the clever use of limited space was innovative. The designs of the fittings were functional, while fussy, old-fashioned interiors dating from the interwar period were replaced with utilitarian design and minimal decoration.

Tarran prefabs in winter, in Killamarsh, North Derbyshire.

Although prefabs had a similar design, came equipped the same way, and were temporary, residents made them their own. Once tenants were allocated their new home, the first thing they had to do was to put up some curtains. Prefabs proved so popular that if one had no curtains, people would think it was available and would harass the housing officers to get it!

Most residents had no money and no possessions because they had been made homeless by the war, or had been living with their in-laws or in furnished rooms. Nevertheless, they still had to purchase items such as beds, a dining table, and chairs, and sometimes had to wait for weeks to get help from the government in the form of essential coupons or 'dockets' for utility purchases.

Just after the war, the available choice of goods in department stores was limited. In 1942, the government set up the Utility Furniture Scheme to cope with the shortages of raw materials and to ration consumption. Utility furniture was originally supplied to those who had been bombed out or who were setting up a new home. Sixty coupons were allocated to each eligible person, who decided how to use them. For example, a chair was one

docket and a wardrobe was eight. The furniture was solidly constructed, plain, functional, well detailed, and made of oak or mahogany.

Designer Gordon Russell was appointed to the scheme by the Utility Furniture Advisory Committee, and he saw it as a way to show the public the benefits of 'good' design. The Board of Trade proposed that the scheme should be 'influencing popular taste towards good construction in simple, agreeable designs to the benefit of our after-the-war homes'. The standardisation and mass production of the Utility Furniture scheme makes an interesting parallel with the Temporary Housing Programme. Like the prefabs, it provided an opportunity for the government to educate the public towards 'better taste'.

Rationing of furniture ended in June 1948, but Utility Furniture continued to be produced. However, in January 1953, the Conservative government ended the scheme. Despite the noble intentions of the Utility scheme to show people the virtues of good design, and later in 1946,

AIROH living room, late 1940s, St Fagans National History Museum, Wales. It has its original cupboards, door and 'window' linked to the kitchen.

The AIROH 'front bedroom' at St Fagans – these rooms were normally used as the children's bedroom.

through the successful Britain Can Make It exhibition, people managed with whatever they could get. Valerie Sommerville, who lived in a prefab in Catford for ten years, recalls: 'I can remember our first carpet – my grandmother bought army surplus grey blankets and she machined them all together in a quilted pattern and put green bindings on the edges, and we only ever had these carpets in the bedrooms.'

The garden and the surrounding space around each detached house contributed to the success of the prefab. It was the perfect balance – living close but not too close to your neighbours. Initially, most of the garden was used to grow fruit and vegetables. Doreen Wallace's 1940 book *How to Grow Food* helped people adapt to wartime and the post-war period, and the successful 'Dig For Victory' campaign was still on everybody's mind. Many grew their own fruit including apples, raspberries, gooseberries, loganberries, strawberries, and blackcurrants.

Just after the war, people bottled preserves at every opportunity, in case supplies ran out. Some residents also kept chickens and rabbits. By the early 1950s, with the fear of hunger diminishing, some prefab tenants would convert

Janet Mackay stands proud in her prefab garden, Paisley, Scotland.

After the war, prefab tenants used most of their outdoor space to grow fruits and vegetables. (AIROH back garden, St Fagans.)

a portion of their garden into a play area for the children, or for roses, begonias, lobelia, and alyssum. Slowly, front gardens became lawns and flowerbeds, a sign of recovery and relative prosperity.

Gardening became a common hobby among prefab residents. The way estates were laid out, with footpaths and alleys, encouraged people to look at their neighbours' achievements and compete. Garden competitions blossomed

A housewife outside her uni-seco prefab, Excalibur Estate, Catford, c. 1950.

Children outside their uni-seco prefab on the Excalibur Estate.

among estate residents. There was competition among the community, but also at a wider local level. It wasn't long before gnomes, wishing wells, and statues appeared on the scene, contributing to a passion for the garden which is still blooming.

Street party on the Treberth Estate, Newport, c. 1950.

Children outside their ARCON prefab, Treberth Estate, c. 1950.

Lord West of Spithead spent his childhood in a prefab in Rosyth, Scotland, in the 1950s, and recalls: 'My father used to sit at the head of the table in the dining room and place his palms on the walls each side and refer to it as his castle. I used to enjoy (when my parents were not around) exiting from the dining room over the roof and back in through my parents' bedroom.'

Guidelines were provided to show how to assemble and use the prefab, and there were also instructions given by the government on how to display the houses. The memorandum for local authorities from the Ministry of Health/Works in 1944 reads: 'The bungalows may be erected on either temporary sites or permanent housing sites. On the temporary sites the land will revert to its present use or will be used later for other than housing purposes. The development works may then have no permanent values and will in most cases have to be demolished. Where the site is to be used as permanent housing in the future, the development works will have been designed or should now be designed to have permanent value.'

It was up to local authorities to decide how and where they would put up the prefabs. Depending on the land and its future use, there were two options. If the prefabs were considered to be temporary, their location was of minor significance, and mainly resulted in rows of identical houses. However, if the local authorities had plans to use the land for permanent housing schemes in the future, they would put an effort in to where the prefabs were built, seeing them as precursors of permanent dwellings. Temporary sites were usually pieces of land that were not intended for housing: they could be bombsites, recreation land, vacant infill lands, and even improbable places like cemeteries!

Lord West in front of the prefab he grew up in in Rosyth, Scotland, about 1954.

South-east London – Elephant and Castle, Peckham, Nunhead, and Dulwich – for example, had many rows or groups of prefabs erected where there was space available. Where permanent housing was envisaged, estates tended to be bigger and their layout much more elaborate, with a mixture of road frontage and footpath access and alleys. Some estates had greens, crescents, and community halls, and some prefabs were erected in staggered rows to break uniformity and display their modern corner windows.

In 1945, when Clement Atlee's Labour government took over, it pursued the Temporary Housing Programme with the same enthusiasm, giving it an even more socialist component. It was the spirit of '45. The NHS was about to be created, and health and housing were the priorities of the new government. People who were allocated prefabs came from the same working-class background, and were mainly either ex-servicemen or had been made homeless during the war. They were of the same generation and often had at least one young child. This contributed to a shared sense of community. Eddie O'Mahony recalled: 'My wife Ellen and I and our two boys were the third family to arrive on the estate in Catford. We had hardly arrived in our prefab when our neighbours came with a tray of tea, sugar, milk, and biscuits. We were very touched as tea was rationed at the time. We were friends for years.'

It was also an era of reconstruction. Hope and optimism were in the air. The nation had suffered but was glorious and victorious. There was a general feeling that everything was possible. The prefab estates became lands of opportunity for those moving from rooms they had to rent and even share in terraced Victorian houses. With the prefabs, a new way of life was born.

Despite the restrictions on post-war life, the prefab represented an ideal life: people were experiencing new technologies together, and even rationing was shared.

Aerial view of the Shrublands Estate, Norfolk, 1962.

During the war, people were united and kept on being so during the post-war years. For the first time in British history, there was real uniformity and standardisation. 'We are all middle-class now,' said politicians: the war had certainly blurred the class lines.

Aerial shot of the Excalibur Estate, Catford.

The unique circumstances that brought together hundreds of people in these identical houses formed strong community bonds. Eddie O'Mahony felt this keenly: 'It was Christmas 1946: something went wrong and people who only had electricity couldn't cook Christmas dinner. This block where I live, we had both gas and electricity and a gas stove. My wife and I said, "Bring the turkeys, your chickens or whatever you want to us and we'll cook them for you." That was the spirit in this estate, all helping one another.'

Children grew up and played together in car-free roads and alleys. The layouts of prefab estates offered a perfect playground and made it easy for parents to look after their children and their neighbours' ones, too. It was like living permanently in a Butlin's holiday village.

Crime rates were very low and resident satisfaction was unusually high. On some estates, people realised that keys opening a prefab door would also fit most of the other ones, but they didn't bother to change them. Also, living in a prefab estate on the outskirts of town, bordering farmland, was a move towards a rural life, which was particularly idealised at the time. This meant moving away from the slums and war-torn towns and city centres. Valerie Sommerville recalls: 'It was very much a community spirit. We had all walks of life here, as people were bombed out, so you had school teachers, park keepers, and there was even a solicitor. Everyone got on with each other.'

'What happened is we got married and left Newport to live in the valley for a long time, twenty-seven years,' recalls Diane Page. 'Alan's dad was left on his own in the prefab. We said, "You've got to come and live with us." But he didn't want to leave his prefab. So we said, "All right then, what if we come down and live with you?" So that's what we did and we bought the prefab.'

'Why do most prefab residents love their homes so much?' is the underlying question of this book. After talking to residents and experts, and reading and researching about the attachment and love for the prefab, a few reasons emerged – the social, political, and historical context; the design and architecture of the prefab; the estate layouts; the communities they helped create; the idea of the reward to servicemen who fought for victory; the quality they provided; and finally, the preservation of a memory – the temporary housing measure turned into a never-ending love story.

Street party in the 1980s on the Excalibur Estate, Catford. There are many examples of generations of families who lived or still live together on the same estate.

SEVENTY YEARS ON

INSTEAD OF THE 500,000 prefabs Churchill had announced, only 156,000 were built under the Temporary Housing Programme (THP). They ended up costing more than expected, while traditional houses were actually cheaper to build. However, more than 250,000 houses which involved some degree of prefabrication were built in the late 1940s and in the beginning of the 1950s. The country still lacked sufficient housing, and prefabrication was the only way to offer a quick solution. But by this time, the houses were considered and designed to be permanent. Their production and assembly also helped to get unskilled workers into employment.

Two semi-attached BL8 prefabs in Chesterfield.

This is when system building – where factory-made panels were attached to a framework on site – was born and became increasingly common. Permanent prefabs were sometimes slightly bigger (with a third bedroom) and semi-detached or double-storey, and they were as much loved by their tenants as the THP ones.

Some of the different post-war permanent prefabs include the BL8 aluminium bungalows. Designed and manufactured by the Bristol Aircraft Company from the late 1940s to 1953, they were sometimes also known as the Hawksley bungalows, because some were sold by Hawksley Constructions Ltd. BL8 prefabs were available in detached and semi-detached forms; the semi-detached version was the most popular. They are slightly bigger than THP prefabs and have an additional room. There are still some BL8s in Redditch, northeast Worcestershire, and in Chesterfield, Derbyshire.

The London County Council (LCC) Mobiles, built from 1963 to 1967, were designed by Hubert Bennett and manufactured by Calders of County Durham. They retailed at £1,239 and were put up in East and South London (Limehouse, Stepney, Blackfriars, Elephant and Castle, New Cross, and Plumstead). They had asbestos walls with a dark-stained cedar trim and a flat roof, and

LCC prefabs in Kennington, London, 1973.

were often built in small numbers on bombsites. The LCC layout was similar to the THP prefabs, but they were much smaller. A three-bedroom version existed with the extra bedroom sticking out awkwardly at the rear. The last LCCs were pulled down in the late 1990s.

BISF house in Corby, Northamptonshire.

British Iron and Steel Federation houses (BISF) were designed by architect Frederick Gibberd and engineer Donovan Lee in 1943. About 30,000 went up in Yorkshire. They were double storey, had a steel frame, and light pressed-steel sheets. Many of the BISF houses are still standing and are in good condition.

The Airey house, built in 1947, was designed and manufactured by William Airey & Sons in Leeds. About 20,000 were built across the country. There were two varieties: the flat-roofed 'rural' and the pitched-roof 'urban', built using precast concrete panels, and they were usually double storey.

The Scottwood dates back to the 1940s. It was designed by Hubert Scott-Paine, an aircraft and boat

An Airey prefab in Chinnor, Oxfordshire, with later replacement windows. The house to the left would once have looked much the same, but has been updated with brick cladding.

designer and inventor. Timber panels were used in their construction, they were clad with plywood, and filled with glass-fibre insulation. Scottwoods had two storeys and were mostly put up in South London and Southampton, but none remain.

Swedish houses in Leverburgh, Harris, Scotland.

Swedish houses were originally designed both in Sweden and Finland in the 1940s then slightly redesigned for the British market. About five thousand were imported. They were made from heavy timber panels, and had outer and inner sheathing. They were single or double storey. They were designed so unskilled labourers could assemble the houses. Some still survive in very good condition on Lewis and Harris in the Outer Hebrides, as well as in other parts of Scotland, Doncaster, Kent and Hampshire.

By 1949, it was up to local authorities to decide the future of the prefabs. Small clusters that were built near a town centre were more likely to be pulled down than the large, established estates. Some local authorities followed new ideas on social housing design. The government encouraged them to use system building and non-traditional construction that required less skilled labour.

From the beginning of the 1960s, the focus of the local authorities shifted from suburban estates to inner cities. Social housing meant higher-density buildings.

The era of tower blocks was born. Although flats became the new model of modern social housing, they were not as successful as the prefabs; they never became the new palaces for the people. In fact, few of the house types that succeeded the prefabs attracted the same admiration from residents. People wanted detached homes, gardens, and well-designed interiors full of light – features that a flat in a tower block could never offer.

Margaret Thatcher's time in office (1979–90) was bracketed by two major housing acts – in 1980 and 1988 – that fundamentally changed the UK housing system. For Thatcher, home ownership meant a cohesive and moral family life. Reliance upon social housing was viewed as sapping personal responsibility and initiative, and Thatcher made the right to buy council housing a Conservative Party policy.

Some 7,000 council houses were sold to tenants during 1970, but that figure soared to more than 45,000 by 1972. After Margaret Thatcher became Prime Minister in 1979, the legislation to implement the right to buy was passed in the Housing Act 1980. It gave tenants the right to buy their council house at a discount, depending on how long they had lived in the house and on its market value.

In the following decade more than a million council homes were sold and the majority of sold-off homes were not replaced. Prefabs, even if classified as temporary, could be bought under the right-to-buy scheme, like any other social housing. Graham Burton, owner of a Tarran in North Wingfield, North Derbyshire, revealed: 'I bought my prefab in 1991. It cost me £11,000 at the time', and owner Barbara Rollinson, in Old Brampton, Chesterfield, North Derbyshire, bought her prefab for £8,000 in the 1990s, as well as a piece of personal history – she was born in the main room in 1948.

Since the 1990s, people have carried on buying up prefabs, but this hasn't guaranteed their safety.

Graham Burton bricked up his Tarran for better insulation, and added a conservatory at the back.

Local authorities can redevelop the lands they were erected on. Lewisham Council, in south-east London, for example, has used compulsory purchase orders to buy privately owned prefabs.

Decades of underinvestment during both Conservative and Labour administrations had left more than half of all social tenant households (2.3 million) living in unfit homes in England, and a revival of prefabrication and mass production was inevitable. John Prescott, deputy Prime Minister from 1997 to 2007, was concerned about young people being priced out of the house market. He challenged the construction industry to build homes for just £60,000.

Barbara Rollinson was born in this prefab in Old Brampton in 1948, and bought it in the 1990s.

For Prescott, prefabrication or 'modern methods of construction' went alongside urban densification. Ideas for micro-flats and stackable Modular Housing Systems were encouraged in order to get more residential units on to ever more expensive land. But the new prefabricated

Grade II listed
Phoenix prefabs
in Moseley,
Birmingham.

building methods and Prescott's scheme met with criticism and remained an experiment.

As more and more prefabs disappeared, English Heritage considered listing some of them in the early 1990s. English Heritage historian Julian Holder suggested listing each type: 'Where good examples do occur particular attention should be paid to the quality and completeness of the fixtures and fittings. The difference within each type should also be considered together with the possibility of identifying early prototypes.'

As a result, Grade II status was given to sixteen Phoenix prefabs on Wake Green Road, in Moseley, Birmingham in 1998, as well as to two pairs of Swedish timber frame houses in Spittlerush Lane, Doncaster in 2003, and to six prefabs on the Excalibur Estate in Catford in 2009. The Grade II listing given to the prefabs acknowledges their historic interest, but it doesn't save them from demolition. It is the local authorities that have the last word.

REGENERATION PROJECTS AND TWENTY-FIRST-CENTURY PREFABS

THE KIND OF housing that replaced the prefabs depended on the time they were pulled down, the type of land they were built on, the size of the estate, the determination of the residents to keep them, and the local authority's policies. Usually, prefabs were replaced with bungalows or small blocks, using traditional building materials and methods, as well as system building.

This Arcon in Newport, Wales, is one of the last three Arcons still standing and lived in.

In 2002 this brick bungalow was built to replace an Arcon in Newport, Wales.

In Newport and North Derbyshire, housing associations and local authorities developed regeneration programmes with a participative approach. In Newport, when the decision was taken to regenerate the Treberth and Bishpool prefab estates in the early 2000s, the residents had the choice between keeping their old prefab or opting for a new brick bungalow on the same estate. If they went for the second option, they could choose between four different designs, which were all as similar as possible to the old prefabs. Residents also had a say in their new location on the estate. More than a decade after the regeneration project started, there are only three prefabs left. Although the residents were very attached to their prefabs, almost everyone chose to have a new bungalow.

In North Derbyshire, sadly, residents did not have the option to choose between their prefab and a new bungalow. However, the regeneration projects in Killamarsh and Eckington, about fifty prefabs on each estate, were led in a participative way. Residents were involved in the design

Alan Mason led the 2002 campaign to save thirty BL8 bungalows in Redditch.

of the new bungalows, and chose where they would be rehoused on the estate.

One of the reasons many prefabs have lasted this long is the valiant campaigns organised by residents to save their homes from demolition. In 2002, the campaign by Alan Mason and his neighbours in Redditch, northeast

The demolition in 2013 of this Tarran prefab in Eckington, North Derbyshire only took twenty minutes.

Worcestershire, saved thirty BL8 bungalows from demolition. Sadly, not all campaigns are successful. In Catford, Jim Blackender led the campaign to save the 186 Uni-Seco prefabs on the Excalibur Estate from demolition but lost in 2010, and moved out of his prefab in 2012.

In the 1950s, prefabrication was synonymous with temporary. Today, prefabs are made to last, their industrial manufacturing is widespread, and people seek them out. There are even sophisticated prefabs like the German Huf Haus. Prefabricated developments have also appeared on programmes such as Channel 4's *Grand Designs*.

When Lord Kinnock visited the Excalibur Estate in 2013, his view was this: 'If you build prefabs now, you'd be talking about a relatively low occupational price and a low maintenance cost and that all makes a terrific difference to people's standard of living.' He also added that more prefabs should be made today – not only to provide good homes, but also to create jobs in factories.

More than sophisticated, the Huf Haus prefabricated houses are groundbreaking, highly advanced in terms of thermal values, and use alternative energy technologies.

Since the end of the 1990s, the different attempts to use new types of prefabs have been unsuccessful. One-off projects such as the BoKlok flats in Gateshead, the Murray Grove block of flats in Hackney, London, and the Yorkon prefab housing units in York did not get developed or reproduced on a larger scale. Nevertheless, there are still some attempts to build more prefabricated houses or blocks of flats, such as the ten-home scheme developed by Rational House in Hammersmith & Fulham, London.

Undoubtedly off-site construction offers benefits – higher quality, lower wastage, faster construction, and better airtightness – but this doesn't cost less than traditional housing. The major advantage of prefabs as affordable housing is the amount of time they take to be put together.

Today's prefabs, except for the very expensive ones, are rarely seen as 'palaces for the people'. The UK is suffering from a severe housing crisis, but there is no plan to build considerably more social housing. Brenda Vale, Professor at the School of Architecture at the Victoria University of Wellington in New Zealand and author of *A History of the UK Temporary Housing Programme*, probably gives the best analysis why prefabs haven't proved to be the solution to the UK housing crisis:

I haven't yet seen any evidence that the costs stack up such that modern prefabs could address current housing problems. That said, the building process as a whole is much more prefabricated and based on on-site assembly of pre-made parts, and this does seem to work economically. So there is concealed prefabrication going on. In any life-cycle analysis of buildings the energy used to operate a building over its life is still the dominant quantity and any savings in waste that might come from prefabrication are very, very small in comparison, so there have to be other reasons for prefabricating – not yet proven.'

PREFABS TO VISIT

As most of the post-war prefabs are about to disappear, it's time to go and have a look at them. The Excalibur Estate in Catford is the largest remaining collection of prefabs, but not for long as it faces demolition within the next few years. In Peckham (Costa Street), Nunhead (Ivydale Road) and Dulwich (Lordship Lane), a few are still standing. The Treberth and Bishpool Estates in Newport have three original prefabs. Demolition started in 2013 in Killamarsh and Eckington but there are still a few other pockets of Tarrans in Chesterfield, North Wingfield. In Bolsover, not very far from Chesterfield, there are two surviving prefabs that were saved from demolition a few years ago. Brick walls have been added and they look very nice.

A 'done-up' Tarran prefab in Bolsover.

For those who want to see prefabs as they were, some were saved and rebuilt in open-air museums across Britain. Their interiors have been carefully refurbished and arranged, and can be viewed.

St Fagans National History Museum in Wales has an AIROH B2, www.museumwales.ac.uk/en/stfagans/buildings/prefabs

Imperial War Museum in Duxford, Cambridgeshire, has a Uni-Seco, www.iwm.org.uk/collections/item/object/30084361

Chiltern Open Air Museum in Buckinghamshire has a Universal, www.coam.org.uk/index.php/about-us/historic-buildings/amersham-prefab

Avoncroft Museum in Bromsgrove, Worcestershire has an Arcon Mark V, www.avoncroft.org.uk/about-us

Eden Camp Modern History Theme Museum in Malton, North Yorkshire, has a Tarran, www.edencamp.co.uk/prefab.html

Rural Life Centre, in Farnham, Surrey, has an Arcon Mark V, www.rurallife.plus.com/rurallife

The listed prefabs on Wake Green Road in Moseley, Birmingham, are worth a visit, as well as the prefabs in Redditch, northeast Worcestershire, and in Plasterfield, Stornoway. The Isle of Lewis also counts dozens of Swedish houses in Stornoway and Leverburgh. They are still in a very

A small prefab estate in Paisley, Scotland.

An episode of *Rock & Chips*, prequel to *Only Fools and Horses*, being shot on the Excalibur Estate, Catford.

good state and look picturesque in the beautiful Hebrides landscape. Near Glasgow, in Paisley, two lovely estates of prefabs are still standing and don't seem under threat.

Correspondence with prefab residents and enthusiasts suggest there are many more prefabs in other towns

Artist Bobby Baker's installation, *Edible Family in a Mobile Home*, 1976.

and cities. There is a Facebook page – facebook.com/PalacesforthePeople – which aims to keep alive the memory of post-war prefab life through gathering and sharing images and films, documents and stories, and encouraging discussions, research, and projects about prefabs. The website maps the location of the remaining post-war prefabs in the UK and also where they once stood.

It is not surprising that after so many years of existence, other uses have been found for prefabs too. Some have been converted into garages, workshops, or temporary accommodation for farmers. Others have even been part of artistic projects such as the LCC prefabs used by Acme Studios in Hackney in the 1970s. These are only a few examples of curious prefab facts. There are probably many more to be discovered in the UK and even abroad.

David Willis's 1:12 scale model of a Uni-Seco, 2014.

FURTHER READING

Arieff, Allison, and Burkhart, Bryan. *Prefab*. Gibbs M. Smith Inc, 2003.

Bullock, Nicholas. *Building the Post-War World*. Routledge, 2002.

Casson, Hugh. *Homes by the Million*. Penguin Books, 1946.

Davies, Colin. *The Prefabricated Home*. Reaktion Books, 2005.

Finnimore, Brian. *Houses from the Factory: System Building and the Welfare State*. Rivers Oram Press, 1989.

Gossel, Peter. *Prefab Houses*. Taschen, 2014.

Herbers, Jill. *Prefab Modern*. Harper Design, 2006.

Holyoake, Gregory. *The Prefab Kid: A Postwar Childhood in Kent*. SB Publications, 1998.

Kaufmann, Michelle, and Remick, Cathy. *Prefab Green*. Gibbs Smith, 2009.

Robins, Gary. *Prefabrications*. Pfotogallery, 2001.

Sked, Alan, and Cook, Chris. *Post-war Britain: a Political History, 1945–1992*. Penguin History, 1993.

Smith, Ryan. *Prefab Architecture: a Guide to Modular Design and Construction*. John Wiley & Sons, 2011.

Stevenson, Greg. *Palaces for the People: Prefabs in Postwar Britain*. Batsford, 2003.

Tarpey, Paul. *More Prefab Days: Belle Vale Remembers*. Enterprise Marketing and Publishing Services Ltd, 2008.

Vale, Brenda. *The History of the UK Temporary Housing Programme*. Taylor & Francis, 1995.

INDEX